BABY ANIMALS

Published by Creative Education, Inc., 123 South Broad Street, Mankato, Minnesota 56001

Printed by permission of Wildlife Education, Ltd.

ISBN 0-88682-270-X

BABY ANIMALS

Created and Written by
John Bonnett Wexo

Zoological Consultant
Charles R. Schroeder, D.V.M.
Director Emeritus
San Diego Zoo &
San Diego Wild Animal Park

Scientific Consultants
Mark S. Rich, M.S.
Curator of Mammals
San Diego Zoo

Arthur Crane Risser, Ph.D.
Curator of Birds
San Diego Zoo

Charles R. Schroeder, D.V.M
San Diego Zoo

Photographic Credits

Front Cover: Zig Leszczynski *(Animals Animals)*; **Pages Six and Seven:** Norman R. Lightfoot *(Photo Researchers)*; **Page Six: Upper Right,** Marc and Evelyne Bernheim *(Woodfin Camp)*; **Page Seven: Upper Left,** Charles G. Summers, Jr. *(Bruce Coleman, Inc.)*; **Upper Right,** Ira Block *(Woodfin Camp)*; **Center Left,** Stouffer Productions *(Animals Animals)*; **Center Right,** 1981© Peter B. Kaplan; **Lower Right,** Peter Veit; **Page Eight: Center Left,** Marvin E. Newman *(Woodfin Camp)*; **Lower Left,** Bill Strode *(Woodfin Camp)*; **Upper Right,** Zig Leszczynski *(Animals Animals)*; **Center Right,** Donna Grosvenor *(Woodfin Camp)*; **Page Nine: Upper Left,** Loren McIntyre *(Woodfin Camp)*; **Lower Left,** Kevin Jackson *(Animals Animals)*; **Upper Right,** Charles G. Summers Jr. *(Bruce Coleman, Inc.)*; **Lower Right,** Loren McIntyre *(Woodfin Camp)*; **Pages Ten and Eleven:** M. Phillip Kahl *(Photo Researchers)*; **Page Ten: Center Left,** Jack Couffer *(Bruce Coleman, Inc.)*; **Upper Right,** Ian Beames *(Ardea)*; **Page Eleven: Upper Right,** Dinny Slaughter *(Photo Researchers)*; **Lower Left,** Joanna Van Gruisen *(Ardea)*; **Page Twelve: Lower Left,** David C. Fritts *(Animals Animals)*; **Upper Right,** Donna Grosvenor *(Woodfin Camp)*; **Bottom Center,** Souricat *(Animals Animals)*; **Page Thirteen: Upper Left,** Stephen J. Krasemann *(Photo Researchers)*; **Upper Right,** Jonathan Blair *(Woodfin Camp)*; **Center Left,** Jim Brandenburg *(Woodfin Camp)*; **Center Right,** Esao Hashimoto *(Animals Animals)*; **Lower Left,** David C. Fritts *(Animals Animals)*; **Pages Fourteen and Fifteen:** John E. Swedberg *(Ardea London)*; **Pages Sixteen and Seventeen:** I. W. Sedgwick *(Animals Animals)*; **Page Sixteen: Center Left,** Susan McCarthy *(Photo Researchers)*; **Lower Left,** Zig Leszczynski *(Animals Animals)*; **Page Seventeen: Upper Center,** Leonard Lee Rue III *(Bruce Coleman Inc.)*; **Upper Right,** Jonathan Blair *(Woodfin Camp)*; **Lower Right,** Oxford Scientific Films *(Animals Animals)*; **Pages Eighteen and Nineteen:** Leonard Zorn *(Animals Animals)*; **Page Twenty: Lower Left,** Martin Rogers *(Woodfin Camp)*; **Upper Right,** 1981© Peter B. Kaplan; **Lower Right,** Jim Brandenburg *(Woodfin Camp)*; **Page Twenty-one: Lower Left,** Donna Grosvenor *(Woodfin Camp)*; **Upper Right,** Martin Rogers *(Woodfin Camp)*: **Center Left,** E. Hanumantha Rao *(Photo Researchers)*; **Lower Right,** Breck P. Kent *(Animals Animals)*; **Pages Twenty-two and Twenty-Three:** Wendell Metzen *(Bruce Coleman, Inc.)*.

Our Thanks To: Susan Hathaway *(Zoological Society of San Diego)*; Lynnette Wexo.

Creative Education would like to thank Wildlife Education, Ltd., for granting them the rights to print and distribute this hardbound edition.

Contents

Why are babies cute? Scientists tell us that cuteness has definite survival value for many babies, since parents often cannot resist the appealing looks and helpless cries of their offspring. Cute babies are likely to get better care than they might otherwise get.

This seems to be especially true of baby mammals and birds. Like human babies, they often have what it takes to make you love them at first sight—large glowing eyes, big clumsy feet, soft fur or downy feathers, a trusting and helpless look.

African Lion Cub

Harp Seal Pup

Owl Chick

Orangutan

Mule Deer Fawn

Blue-footed Booby

Mountain Gorilla

The world is filled with babies.

The only places that animals are not found on earth are the hottest, coldest, or highest places. Everywhere else, if man has not destroyed their environment, different types of animals live...and have babies.

Some animals occupy a large area, or range, while others are limited to very small areas. But whatever the range may be, the animals who live there are suited to the nature of the land and the climate—and this goes for their babies as well. If it is cold, newborns may have fur. If it is hot, they may be naked. Later on, as the weather changes or they migrate to new areas, they may change to suit new conditions. In general, nature gives every baby the best chance it can to survive, wherever it is born.

Some animals, such as this baby raccoon, benefit from living close to man. They are good at hiding themselves, and they like to eat food that people throw away. Raccoons, skunks, and opossums are often found living in the middle of cities.

The ranges of some animals have been increased a great deal by man. Wherever people go, they bring their farm animals with them. Cows are now found all over the world, in just about every place that is warm enough for farming.

Many animal babies grow up in forests. They are safer up in the trees than they would be on the ground, because fewer animals can catch them. Baby chimpanzees like to swing from branch to branch, and they enjoy eating leaves.

Five hundred years ago, there were no horses in North or South America. They were brought over from Europe by the first settlers, and quickly increased in numbers. Soon, there were almost as many horses as people.

Animal babies can be born in very cold places. These gentoo (JEN-TOO) penguins start life close to the South Pole. Their fuzzy feathers keep them warm, even when they swim in the cold water. They will never fly, because their wings are not big enough—but they will become wonderful swimmers.

In the high mountains, babies must know how to climb. Rocky Mountain goats start jumping around when they are only 30 minutes old. They are born with a sense of balance, and can climb steep slopes when only days old.

High in the mountains of South America, there are flat places where grass grows. Young llamas (YAH-MUZ) start eating grass soon after they are born. Their long shaggy hair keeps them warm in the cool mountain air.

Up near the North Pole, the summers are short. During this brief warm period, Arctic foxes are born. They cannot see for the first few weeks of their lives, so they stay in an underground den. Their mothers stay close to them, and their fathers bring food.

Babies come in all sizes. Some animals are so small at birth that you can hardly see them, while others are so large that it seems strange to call them babies at all. Size is one thing that determines how a baby animal will react when danger threatens. Small babies find it easy to hide, and will usually stand still or scamper for cover. Larger babies, which cannot hide under a leaf, will usually run or will seek the protection of adult animals in a herd.

Mice are very, very tiny when they are born. They weigh only one gram, and have no hair. But they start eating right away and grow very fast. By the time they are three months old, their weight can increase as much as 30 times!

Many animals are much smaller at birth than they will later become. A North American lynx kitten is only a ball of fur that you can hold in your hand. When full grown, it can weigh more than 40 pounds (18 kilograms).

When a baby giraffe is born, it is already as big as a man. It stands 6 feet (183 centimeters) tall, and weighs about 115 pounds (53 kilograms). Young giraffes follow their mothers everywhere, and do everything that their mothers do.

Some animals are small at birth and never grow much bigger. The golden marmoset is about as wide as a man's finger when it is born. When fully grown, it will probably weigh less than 9 ounces (260 grams), and will be only about 8 inches long (200 millimeters).

Some animals start big—and get much bigger. A baby elephant weighs about 200 pounds (91 kilograms) and is over 3 feet (1 meter) tall at birth. When it is fully grown, it may weigh over 10,000 pounds (4536 kilograms) and be more than 9 feet (3 meters) tall.

Some babies get better care

than others, because they need more help to survive. In general, if an animal is going to be guided mostly by instinct as an adult, it will get very little help from its parents. But if it must learn many things in order to be successful as an adult, it will spend more time with its parents.

Fish and reptiles, for example, are usually born with all the physical abilities and knowledge they will need. They don't need much help from their parents, and they don't usually get much. Often, in fact, parents will lay eggs and go away before the young even hatch.

Mammals and birds, on the other hand, must usually learn more skills to live. Often, they are totally helpless at birth and would surely die if their mothers didn't take care of them. As they grow up, they learn from watching their mothers. In nature, baby animals always obey their mothers, because their lives could depend on it.

Baby aoudads (OO-DADS) stay close to their mothers. All members of the aoudad herd watch out for any animals that might try to eat the youngsters.

Female bears are fine mothers. They spend a lot of time teaching their cubs how to catch food, and will fight hard to protect their young from harm. This brown bear mother is showing her cubs how to catch fish, one of a bear's favorite foods.

Young lions like to show their love for their mothers by nuzzling and licking them. Lion cubs may stay with their mothers for several years.

Crocodiles look nasty, but females take very good care of their young. If danger threatens, they will pick up their babies in their mouth and carry them to safety (as shown below).

Sometimes, mother animals must leave their young alone while they search for food. To protect themselves, the babies hide and stay very quiet.

Some animals are good mothers in some ways, and not so good in other ways. Pelicans will bring their babies plenty of fish to eat. But if a predator tries to eat one of their young, pelican mothers may do nothing to protect them.

Young cheetahs must learn how to hunt. Their mother takes them hunting with her, and spends endless hours demonstrating how they should stalk their prey.

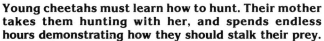

Monkeys can be very good parents. Mother monkeys often carry their babies on their backs, and take them to places where good food is to be found. Like human mothers, they can spend a lot of time cleaning their children and teaching them how to behave.

A mother Polar bear takes good care of her cubs. She will protect them and teach them to swim in the water. The mother bear also teaches her cubs how to catch fish and seals.

Some animals grow up faster than others, because fast growth helps them to survive. The world of a baby animal can be a dangerous place. There are many other animals that would like to eat the small creature, and in many places, if a baby remains helpless for too long, it will surely be eaten. In general, animals born in unprotected places, or whose parents cannot protect them from predators, grow up faster.

Ducks are born ready to go. As soon as they dry off, they are able to walk, swim, and eat solid food. But it takes several months before they are able to fly.

Baby snakes look like small versions of their parents when they hatch. They grow so fast that they may shed their skin seven times during their first year of life to make room for their growing bodies.

Most cats are helpless when they are born. Their eyes do not open for a week or more, and they must stay hidden inside a den for their protection.

Many types of birds are born without feathers. They are unable to move around, and must be protected by their parents for weeks or even months.

Young herd animals, such as zebras, must be able to keep up with the moving herd soon after they are born. If they fall behind, they will almost certainly be eaten by lions or other predators. For this reason, young zebras get up on their feet within minutes after birth. Within an hour, they are able to run.

Some animals, like rabbits, grow up very fast. Rabbits may leave their mothers only 6 weeks after they are born. And within 6 months, they can have babies of their own.

This Great Horned Owl mother keeps a careful watch over her chick. She will soon be bringing insects and mice for his dinner.

The future of baby animals is up to us. Many baby animals will not live to grow up, and many baby animals will not even be born if we do not help. Wild animals have as much right to live as we do, but thoughtless people are destroying the animals by destroying the wild lands in which they live.

People are cutting down trees to make room for houses and farms. People are polluting the air and the water that animals must have to live. People are hunting wild animals and capturing them for no good reason. As a result of all of these things, the numbers of many types of wild animals are getting very small.

Zoos and wildlife groups are doing everything they can to help animals survive in their natural homes — and to help them live in protected areas if their natural homes are totally destroyed. Scientists are doing research to find out what each type of animal must have to live. They are studying ways to increase the number of babies that are born. If we love wild animals and want to have them in our world, we must help scientists and zoos to do all of these things.

No one knows if gorillas will be able to continue living in the wild in Africa. The land where they live is being changed to make room for farms—and there is less and less room for gorillas. Happily, many baby gorillas are being born in zoos, where they will be safe.

For the first 3 or 4 years of their lives, human babies and chimpanzee babies are about equal in their intelligence. Like human infants, young chimps need a lot of attention. They love to play with toys, and chimps in some zoos have playrooms, complete with television sets.

One hundred years ago, the American bison was almost totally destroyed by too much hunting. Just in time, special areas were set aside as bison preserves. After years of protection, the bison herds are growing large again.

In certain ways, baby animals are better off in a zoo than they would be in the wild. They get the same kind of medical care that human babies get, and they are protected from animals that might hunt them in the wild.

A few years ago, it looked as though tigers would die out in the wild. But they are now protected, and in some places they are increasing in numbers.

Many wild animals, like this baby mountain lion, are still in great danger. They will only survive if people stop hunting them and stop destroying the wild lands in which they live.

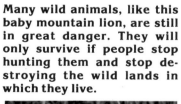

For reasons that no one fully understands, animal mothers in zoos will sometimes refuse to raise their babies. Zoo keepers take over the job and give the babies as much love and care as their mothers would usually give them.

Index